Welcome to the Rain Forest

by Honor Head

Published in 2017 by Ruby Tuesday Books Ltd.

Editors: Jean Coppendale and Mark J. Sachner
Designer: Emma Randall
Consultant: Sally Morgan
Production: John Lingham

Photo credits
Alamy: 28 (left); FLPA: 6 (main), 7 (main), 8, 12, 17 (top left), 19, 20 (right), 23 (bottom), 25 (bottom); Shutterstock: Cover, 2–3, 4–5, 6 (left), 7 (top), 9, 10–11, 13, 14–15, 16, 17 (top right), 17 (bottom), 18, 20 (left), 21, 22, 23 (top), 24, 25 (top), 26–27, 28 (right), 30–31; Superstock: 29.

Library of Congress Control Number: 2017908523

Print ISBN: 978-1-911341-95-6
eBook ISBN: 978-1-911341-96-3

Printed and published in the United States of America

For further information including rights and permissions requests, please contact our Customer Service Department at 877-337-8577.

Contents

Welcome to the Rain Forest 4
On the Rain Forest Floor 6
A Very Wet Habitat 8
Meet the Capybaras 10
HISSSS! 12
A Big Cat in the Forest 14
The Rain Forest Canopy 16
Life in the Canopy 18
Birds and Beaks 20
When Is a Leaf Not a Leaf? 22
Fit for a Frog! 24
Top Trees 26
A Treetop Predator 28
A Rain Forest Food Web 30
Glossary 31
Index, Read More, Learn More Online 32

Words shown in **bold** in the text are explained in the glossary.

Welcome to the Rain Forest

Who and what lives in the wet, hot, steamy Amazon rain forest?

This **habitat** is home to tall trees, ferns, and many other plants.

The animals that live in this habitat include jaguars, birds, and frogs.

Every living thing in the rain forest gets what it needs to live from its habitat.

A rain forest is one of the wettest places on Earth. It is made up of four layers—the forest floor, the understory, the canopy, and the top, or emergent trees. Very little sunlight reaches the ground through the thick trees.

Let's explore the Amazon rain forest floor....

On the Rain Forest Floor

The rain forest floor is dark and damp.

It is covered with a layer of **leaf litter**.

This is made up of fallen trees, branches, leaves, flowers, and fruit.

In the steamy forest, the leaf litter soon rots and becomes part of the soil. The trees take up the **nutrients** they need to be healthy from the soil.

Cup fungi

Fungi feed on the rotting plants.

Millipedes help recycle dead leaves by eating them.

Their poop, which is filled with nutrients, gets mixed into the soil.

An agouti finds a feast of fallen fruit.

What happens to some of the rain that falls on the forest?

A Very Wet Habitat

The rain that falls on the forest creates rivers, lakes, and swampy areas.

Armadillos live on the forest floor near water.

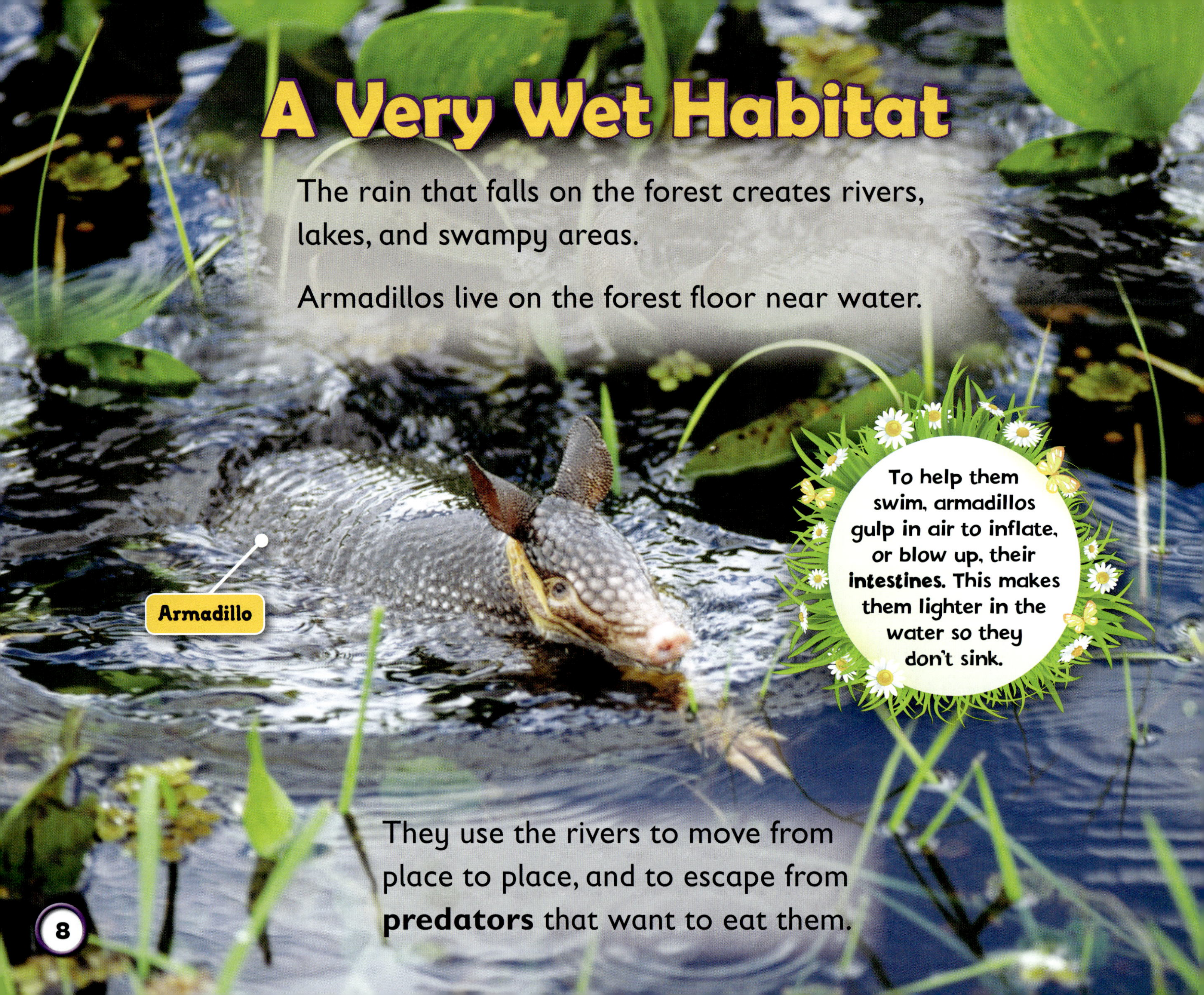

To help them swim, armadillos gulp in air to inflate, or blow up, their **intestines**. This makes them lighter in the water so they don't sink.

They use the rivers to move from place to place, and to escape from **predators** that want to eat them.

Armadillos use their snouts to dig for beetles in the leaf litter.

They also feed on ants and termites.

They have a long, sticky tongue that can slurp up lots of insects at once.

Which forest animal lives on land but has webbed feet?

Meet the Capybaras

Some rain forest animals live both on land and in the water.

Capybaras live on land but are also excellent swimmers and divers.

They use the water to keep cool when it is hot.

Capybaras jump into rivers and lakes to escape from predators, such as snakes and jaguars.
A capybara has webbed feet for swimming. When it dives underwater, it can press its ears against its head to keep the water out.
An adult capybara is the size of a large pig.
Webbed feet
What danger is lurking in the trees that hang over the river?

HISSSS!

Above the forest floor is a tangle of bushes and small trees called the understory.

Huge, brown snakes called anacondas live in the understory.

A female anaconda can grow to be more than 16 feet (5 m) long.

An anaconda hunts on the ground for capybaras.

Its color and patterns make it difficult to see among the plants.

It also slides into the water to catch birds, turtles, and caimans.

Caimans have strong jaws and sharp teeth to fight off anacondas and other predators.

What other hunter wants to have a caiman for dinner?

A Big Cat in the Forest

The jaguar is a top predator in the Amazon rain forest.

It eats capybaras, caimans, and other forest animals–but nothing eats the jaguar!

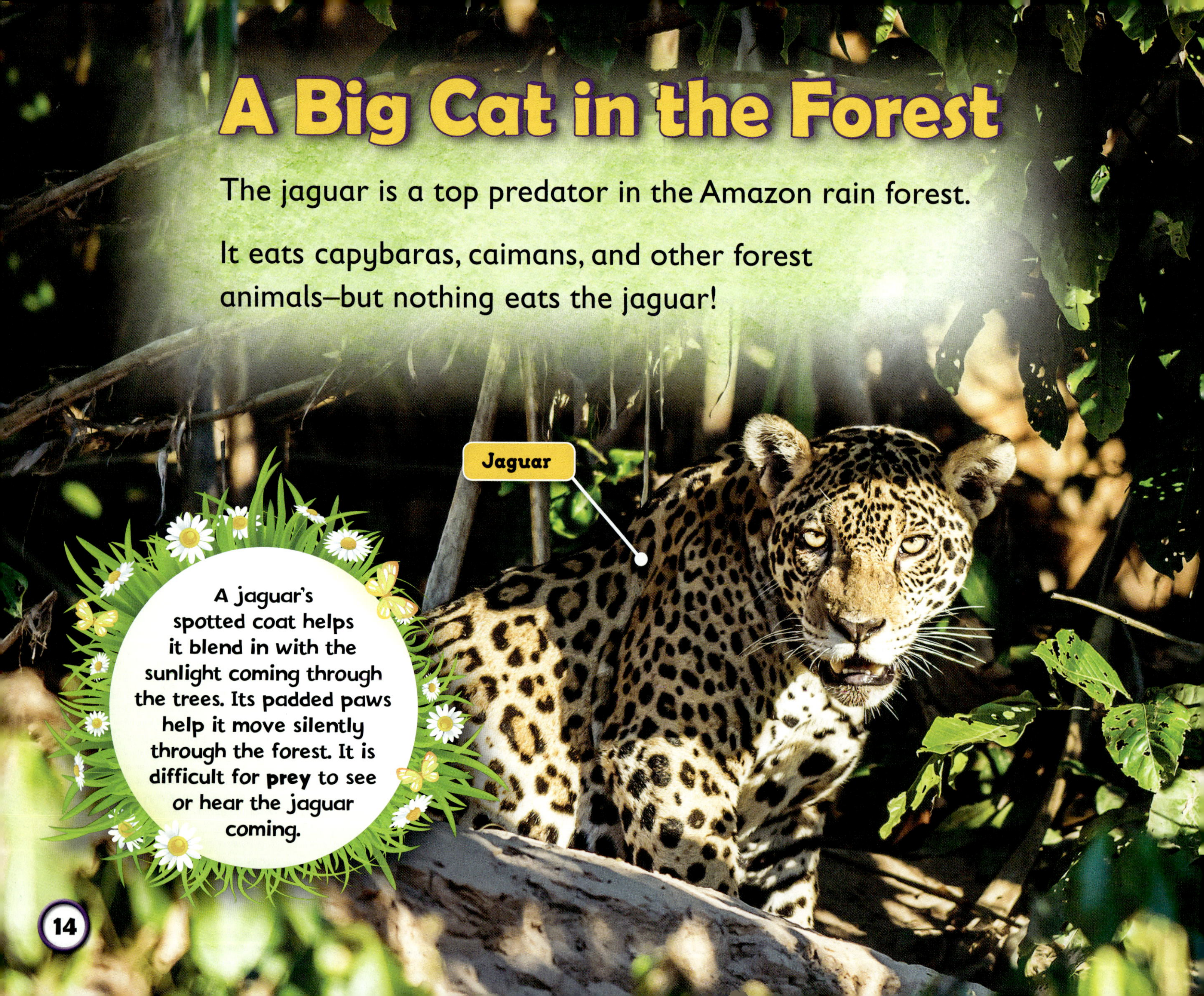

A jaguar's spotted coat helps it blend in with the sunlight coming through the trees. Its padded paws help it move silently through the forest. It is difficult for **prey** to see or hear the jaguar coming.

A jaguar spots a caiman in a river and slips into the water.

She grabs the caiman by the back of its neck.

One strong bite, and the caiman is dead!

Then the jaguar pulls the heavy caiman up the riverbank so she can feed.

What will we find if we climb higher up into the trees?

The Rain Forest Canopy

Above the understory is the green and leafy canopy.

This layer of the forest is made up of the top parts of the trees.

The branches and leaves form a thick, roof-like covering over the forest.

The canopy

A three-toed sloth eating leaves

Nearly all the animals that live in the Amazon rain forest live in the canopy. The trees and other plants provide leaves, flowers, nuts, and berries for them to eat.

The trees are home to ferns, bromeliads, and tiny moss plants.

One tree can have thousands of other plants growing on its trunk and branches.

What animal is making a loud, howling noise in the canopy?

Life in the Canopy

Howler monkey

The air is filled with howls, shrieks, and screams.

These noises are monkeys communicating with each other.

Squirrel monkey

The howl of a howler monkey can be heard for many miles across the forest.

Monkeys sleep, find food, and travel around the forest in the trees.

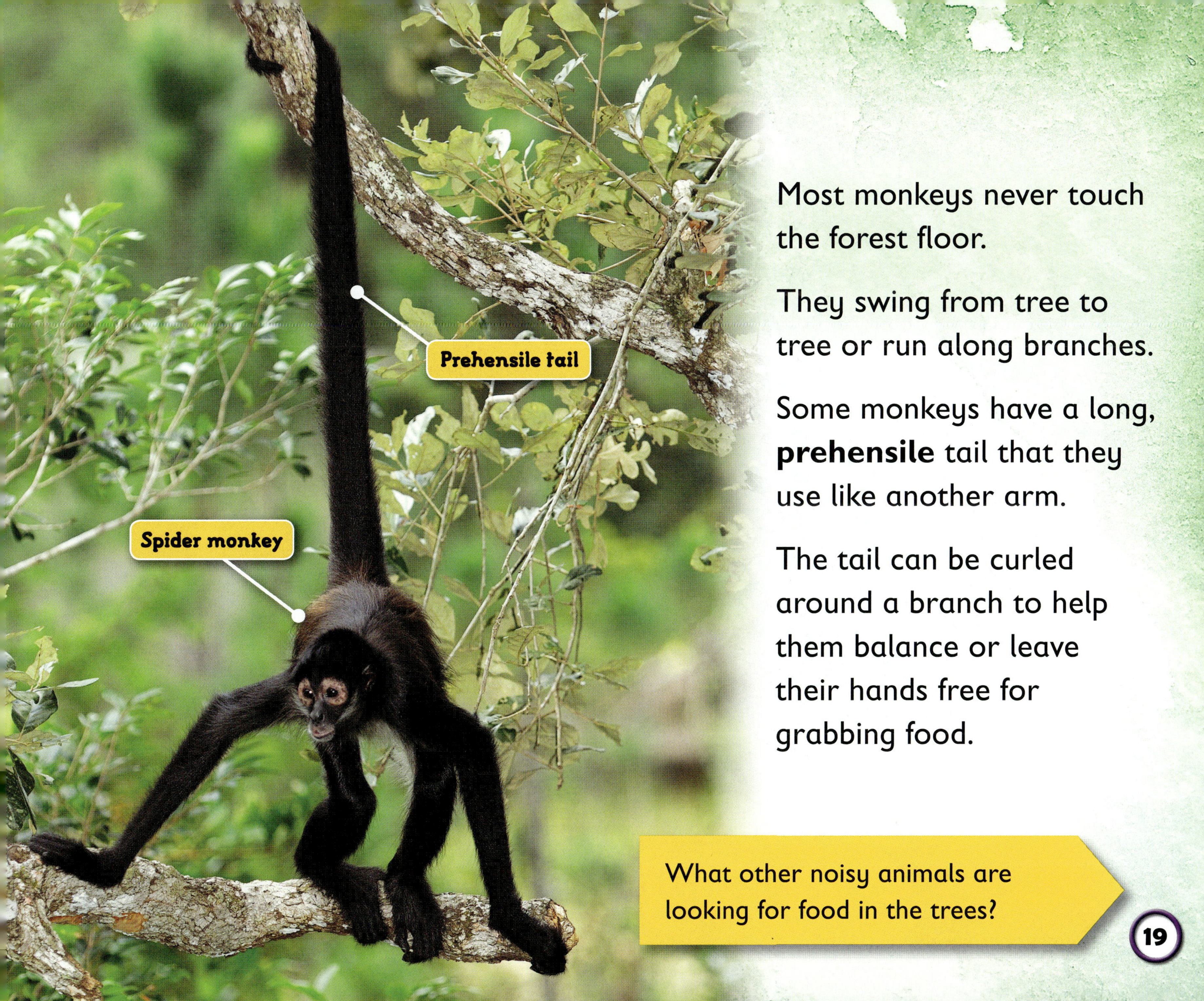

Most monkeys never touch the forest floor.

They swing from tree to tree or run along branches.

Some monkeys have a long, **prehensile** tail that they use like another arm.

The tail can be curled around a branch to help them balance or leave their hands free for grabbing food.

What other noisy animals are looking for food in the trees?

Birds and Beaks

The birds that live in the canopy have a feast of insects, fruit, and nuts to feed on.

They have differently shaped beaks to help them eat their favorite foods.

A toucan uses its long beak to reach for fruit.

A jacamar catches a butterfly in its slim, pointed beak.

A macaw's sharp, hooked beak can split open nuts and fruit.

A sword-billed hummingbird's beak is longer than its body. Its extra-long beak can reach the **nectar** deep inside flowers.

When is a leaf not a leaf?

When Is a Leaf Not a Leaf?

When it is an insect! Some small creatures have developed a way to trick birds and other animals that might want to eat them.

These animals look like a dead leaf or tree trunk that is not very tasty.

Katydid insects look like the leaves of the trees they feed on.

This is called mimicry.

People say katydids make a noise that sounds like someone saying, "Katy did, Katy did." This is how they got their name.

This little tree frog looks like a part of the tree trunk.

This is called camouflage.

What tiny animal uses a bromeliad plant as a swimming pool?

Fit for a Frog!

Some bromeliads have stiff, upright leaves that act like a bowl to collect rainwater.

These little pools of water are very helpful to tiny poison dart frogs.

The frogs lay their eggs on leaves or in damp places.

When tadpoles hatch, the parent frogs carry them up into the towering trees.

They place each tadpole in its own bromeliad.

Inside its tiny pool, the tadpole grows and changes into a frog.

There are lots of rivers and ponds in a rain forest, but these watery places are home to fish and other predators. A bromeliad pool, high up a tree, is a safe place for a tadpole to live.

How high do the tallest rain forest trees grow?

Top Trees

The tallest trees in the rain forest grow above the canopy to form the top, or emergent, layer.

Giant kapok trees grow to over 200 feet (60 m) tall!

Birds, monkeys, and bats live in these trees.

Kapok trees grow flowers that produce seeds in large pods.

Kapok tree flower

The tiny seeds are in white floss that is blown around by the wind.

The seeds float to the ground so new trees can grow.

Bats visit the flowers to feast on nectar. As they feed, the bats become covered with **pollen**. They carry the pollen from tree to tree. This helps the flowers make seeds.

Floss

Seedpod

Seed

Which powerful predator is hunting for monkeys in the treetops?

A Treetop Predator

Harpy eagle

The eagle's wings are nearly 6 feet (2 m) wide.

A harpy eagle is hunting in the treetops.

She uses her super-sharp **talons** and strong legs to snatch a howler monkey from a branch.

Then she carries the monkey back to her nest to feed to her chick.

A pair of harpy eagles build their nest in a kapok tree.

When an eagle finds a branch it wants for its nest, it grabs it with its talons. Then the eagle flaps its wings until the branch breaks off.

An old nest falls down to the forest floor.

Soon the nest rots and becomes part of the leaf litter that feeds the rain forest trees.

A Rain Forest Food Web

A food web shows who eats who in a habitat.

This food web shows the connections between some of the living things in a rain forest.

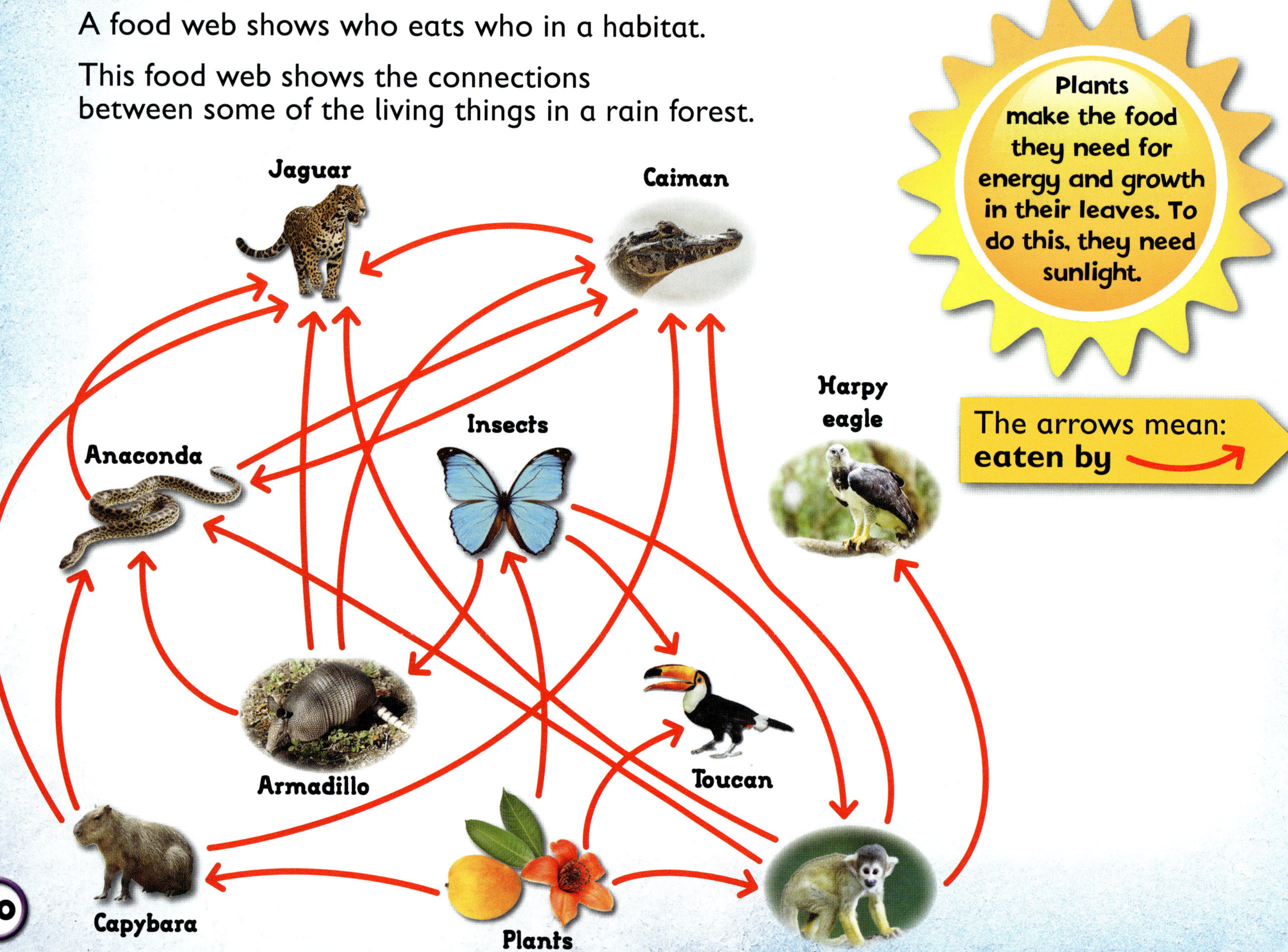

Glossary

fungi (FUHN-jye)
A group of living things that includes mushrooms.

habitat (HAB-uh-tat)
The place where an animal or plant lives. Rain forests, deserts, and gardens are all types of habitats.

intestines (in-TESS-tinz)
Long tubes where an animal's or person's food is digested, or broken down, after it leaves the stomach.

leaf litter (LEEF LIT-ur)
Leaves, twigs, flowers, and fruit that fall to the ground from trees and other plants.

nectar (NEK-tur)
A sugary liquid produced by flowers.

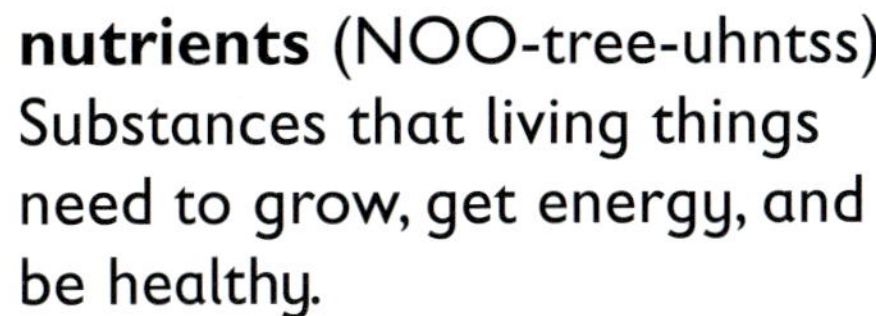

nutrients (NOO-tree-uhntss)
Substances that living things need to grow, get energy, and be healthy.

pollen (POL-uhn)
A colored dust that is made by flowers, and is needed for making seeds.

predator (PRED-uh-tur)
An animal that hunts and eats other animals.

prehensile (pree-HEN-suhl)
Able to grasp or hold on to something.

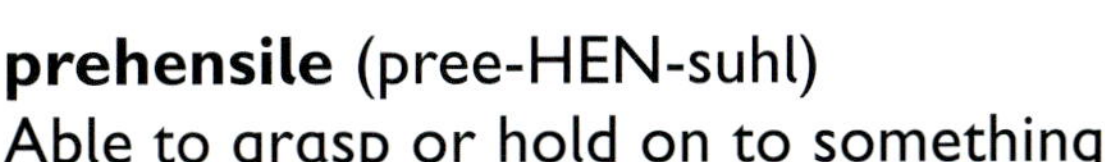

prey (PRAY)
An animal that is hunted by other animals for food.

talons (TAL-uhnz)
Long, sharp claws on the feet of a hunting bird such as an eagle or owl.

Index

A
anacondas 12–13, 30
armadillos 8–9, 30

B
bats 26–27
birds 4–5, 13, 20–21, 22, 26, 28–29, 30
bromeliads 17, 23, 24–25

C
caimans 13, 14–15, 30
canopy 5, 16–17, 18–19, 20, 26
capybaras 10–11, 13, 14, 30

E
emergent layer 5, 26–27

F
ferns 4, 17
flowers 6, 16, 21, 27
forest floor 5, 6–7, 8, 12, 19, 22, 29
frogs 4, 23, 24–25
fruit 6–7, 20–21

H
harpy eagles 28–29, 30

I
insects 9, 20, 22–23, 30

J
jaguars 4, 11, 14–15, 30

K
kapok trees 26–27, 29

L
leaf litter 6–7, 9, 29

M
millipedes 7
monkeys 18–19, 26–27, 28, 30

N
nuts 16, 20–21

P
predators 8–9, 11, 13, 14–15, 20, 22, 25, 27, 28, 30
prey 8–9, 11, 13, 14–15, 20, 22, 25, 28, 30

T
tadpoles 25
turtles 13

U
understory 5, 12, 16

Read More

Lawrence, Ellen. *Jaguar (Apex Predators of the Amazon Rain Forest).* New York: Bearport Publishing (2017).

Owen, Ruth. *Let's Investigate Habitats and Food Chains (Get Started With STEM).* New York: Ruby Tuesday Books (2017).

Learn More Online

To learn more about life in a rain forest, go to
www.rubytuesdaybooks.com/habitats